ORANGE ANIMALS ON THE PLANET

Coloration helps the animals blend into their natural surroundings when they want to hide. While some other species use orange to stand out from the crowd.

ORANGE CLOWNFISH

is widely known as a popular aquarium fish. Orange clownfish can grow to be 11 centimeters in length and can be recognized by three white lines across their bright orange bodies. Orange clownfish often lives in association with sea anemones.

ANDEAN COCK-OF-THE-ROCK

is the national bird of Peru. It is a medium-sized perching bird approximately 32 cm long and weighing 235 g. The Andean cock-of-the-rock is distributed in cloud forests of the Andes.

TIGER

is the largest cat species, reaching a total body length of up to 3.38 m and exceptionally weighing up to 388.7 kg. Its most recognisable feature is a pattern of dark vertical stripes on reddish-orange fur with a lighter underside.

JULIA BUTTERFLY

Its wingspan ranges from 82 to 92 mm, and it is colored orange with black markings. It is native from Brazil to southern Texas and Florida. It is popular in butterfly houses because it is long-lived and active throughout the day.

BABOON SPIDER

is found on the African continent, in Angola, as well as central, eastern, and southern Africa. Female baboon spider can grow to 4–6 inches in size, while males typically range from 3–4 inches. The bite of this species, while not serious, is extremely painful.

ORANGUTAN

Orangutans are among the most intelligent primates; they use a variety of sophisticated tools and construct elaborate sleeping nests each night from branches and foliage. They use large leaves as umbrellas and shelters to protect themselves from the common rains.

JAPANESE SPIDER CRAB

has the greatest leg span of any arthropod, reaching 3.8 metres from claw to claw. The crab is orange, with white spots along the legs. They like to inhabit vents and holes in the deeper parts of the ocean.

RED RIVER HOG

is a wild member of the pig family living in Africa. They typically live in herds of six to 20 members led by a dominant boar. Red river hogs are mostly nocturnal; by day, they hide in dense brush; after sunset, they roam searching for food.

MANED WOLF

is the largest canid
of South America.
The maned wolf also
is known for the
distinctive odor of its
territory markings. Both
female and male maned
wolves use their urine
to communicate.

FLAME ANGELFISH

is bright orange-red with a vertical elongated black spot and four or five bars on the sides. It is found in various reefs of Oceania, most common in Marshall, Line, and Cook Islands.

RED EFT

is a common newt of eastern North America. The bright orange, red-spotted, which is land-dwelling creature is not the creature's adult stage but rather its juvenile iteration. After two or three years, the eft finds a pond and transforms into the aquatic adult.

CORN SNAKE

is a North American species of rat snake. Corn snakes are harmless and beneficial to humans. Corn snakes lack venom and help control populations of wild rodent.

RUDDY SHELDUCK

is a bird of open country, and it will breed on cliffs, in burrows, tree holes or crevices distant from water. The ruddy shelduck is usually found in pairs or small groups and rarely forms large flocks.

ORANGE FLAMINGO

Flamingos' colors can range from pale pink to crimson, depending on the amount of pigment present in the bird's diet. Carotenoid levels in algae and crustaceans vary in different parts of the world, which is why Caribbean flamingos are usually bright red and orange.